YOUR LAND AND MY LAND
The Middle East

We Visit

IRAQ

Claire

O'Neal

Mitchell Lane
PUBLISHERS
P.O. Box 196
Hockessin, Delaware 19707

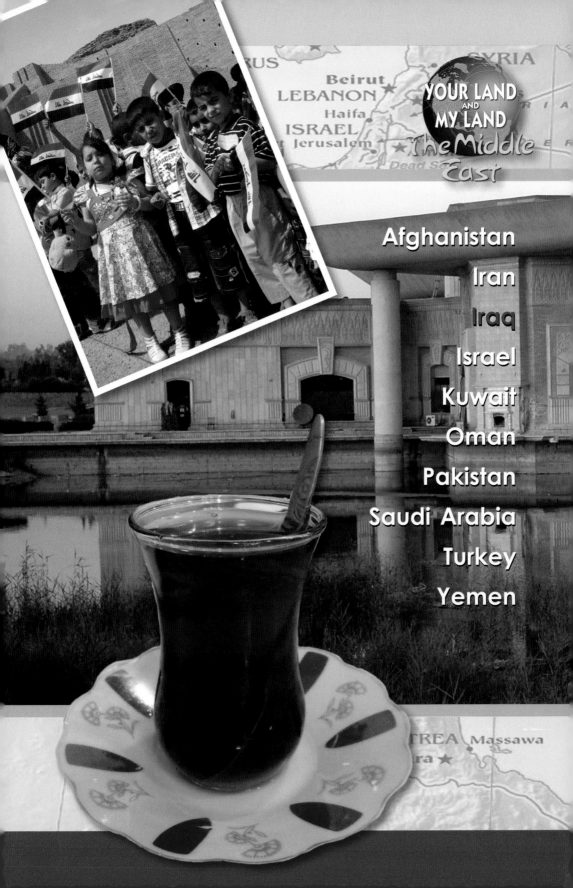

YOUR LAND AND MY LAND
The Middle East

Afghanistan
Iran
Iraq
Israel
Kuwait
Oman
Pakistan
Saudi Arabia
Turkey
Yemen

Kirkuk
Tigris
Baghdad
Kermānshāh
ZAGROS MOUNTA
Qom
Arāk
Eşfahān
RAQ
IRAN
YOUR LAND AND MY LAND
The Middle East
We Visit
IRAQ
Sanaa
YEMEN
Al udaydah
Al Mukalla
Arabia
tasco

Printing   1   2   3   4   5   6   7   8   9

Library of Congress Cataloging-in-Publication Data
O'Neal, Claire.
  We visit Iraq / by Claire O'Neal.
  p. cm. — (Your land and my land: the Middle East)
  Includes bibliographical references and index.
  ISBN 978-1-58415-955-1 (library bound)
  1. Iraq—Juvenile literature. I. Title.
  DS70.62.O54 2012
  956.7—dc23
                                                          2011016771
eBook ISBN: 9781612280974

Contents

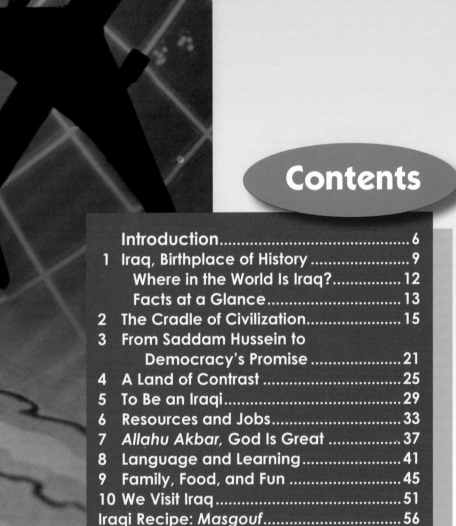

Introduction

The Middle East lies where the lands and peoples of Europe, Asia, and Africa meet. This landscape of contrasts is famous for its punishing, vast deserts, but also boasts towering mountain ranges and sparkling beaches. A natural crossroads, the Middle East has been a center for trade and culture since the dawn of civilization. The major world religions of Judaism, Christianity, and Islam began there. Middle Eastern people share the Arabic language and culture, a reminder that Islam has ruled both hearts and the land since the 700s CE.

A scholar from the Golden Age of Islam would not recognize a map of the Middle East today. After World Wars I and II, European powers carved up the Middle East into countries that would give them control of the region's rich resources, ignoring traditional boundaries used by the ethnic groups that called the land home. Even the term *Middle East* is quite new, coined in 1902 by American naval officer Alfred Mahan as a convenient way to describe the area between the Mediterranean Sea (the "Near East") and India (the "Far East").[1]

Bedouin village

Today, most people know of the Middle East through world headlines that scream of oil and violence. Powerful, ruthless leaders control nearly all Middle Eastern countries. These rulers grow fabulously wealthy on the region's rich resources, leaving most of the population poor and increasingly angry. Iraq sits in the center of the action. With its fertile river valleys, green mountain farmlands, and the world's second-largest oil reserves, people have fought for control of Iraq's beauty and resources for over 5,000 years.

The dome and minaret of the mosque at the Abu Ghurayb (or Ghraib) Presidential Complex. Saddam Hussein built the luxurious complex during the 1990s. It featured extensive water works—using precious water resources while the country's crops withered from drought.

Iraq, Birthplace of History

Welcome to Iraq, the birthplace of history! Over 5,000 years ago, the ancient Sumerians developed the world's first civilization in southeastern Iraq, inventing writing, the calendar, and the wheel. Prophets from the Torah and Bible lived and died there. Najaf and Karbala, two of the holiest shrines in Islam, have attracted visitors for centuries. The capital city, Baghdad, became the center of Islam and world learning in 762 CE, and in 900 CE, it blossomed into the first city anywhere to have more than one million residents.[1]

Iraq's two rivers play a special role in the history of humankind. The Tigris (or *Diljah*) and Euphrates (*al-Furat*) cut lines of lush green across what would otherwise be a desert wasteland. The world's first farms grew out of Mesopotamia, whose Greek name means "Land Between the Rivers." The Garden of Eden may have grown where the rivers meet, near the modern city of al-Qurnah. Today, Iraqis have traded in their plows for oil pumps. The country's petroleum deposits are the world's second largest, and they are the cheapest to produce.

With such richness, however, comes continuous conflict. Throughout history, Mesopotamia has been overrun every few hundred years by the conqueror of the day. Iraq's modern borders, drawn up by the British less than 100 years ago, trap three major ethnic groups in bitter feuds for control of their homelands, the country's oil, and their own religious freedom. Can the rugged Kurds in the north, the conservative Shiite Muslims in the south, and the moderate Sunni Muslims work together to find peace for all Iraqis?

The shrine of Hussein bin Ali in Karbala, Iraq, is one of the holiest places of Shi'a Islam and home to one of the oldest mosques in the world. Muhammad's grandson Hussein is buried there, along with the 72 martyrs that died in battle with him at the Battle of Karbala on October 10, 680 CE.

Where in the World

WHERE IN THE WORLD IS IRAQ?

ISRAEL
West Bank
Amman
Dead Sea (lowest point in Asia, -408 m)
JORDAN
Port Said
Jerusalem
Gaza Strip
Alexandria
Cairo

TURKEY

Cizre
Zakho
Hakkâri
Orūmīyeh
Lake Urmia
Tabrīz
Marāgheh
Miāneh
Zanjī

Urfa
Al Qāmishlī
Dahūk
Āqrah
DAHŪK
Rāyāt
Qal'at Dizah
Mahābād

Al Hasakah
Buhayrat Dahūk
ARBIL
Irbil
AS SULAYMĀNĪYAH

Tall Huqnah
Sinjār
Mosul
NĪNAWĀ
Little Zab
AS SULAYMĀNĪYAH
Halabjah
Sanandaj
Bākhtarān

Dayr az Zawr
Nahr al Khābur
AT TAMĪM
Karkūk
Khānaqīn

SYRIA
Euphrates
Bayjī
Tikrīt
SALĀH AD DĪN
Sāmarrā'
DIYĀLĀ
Ba'qūbah
Mandalī
Īlām
Khorramābād
Borū

Al Qā'im
Buhayrat al Qādisīyah
Hadīthah
Buhayrat ath Tharthār
Ār Ramādī
Al Fallūjah
Baghdad
BAGHDAD
WĀSIŢ
Al Kūt

potash mine
AL ANBĀR
Ar Rutbah
Al Habbānīyah
Buhayrat at Habbānīyah
Bahr al Milh
Karbalā'
BĀBIL
Al Hillah
Al Hayy
Al 'Amārah
MAYSĀN

De facto boundary as shown on official Iraqi and Jordanian maps. (alignment approximate)
Al Hindīyah
KARBALĀ'
Ad Dīwānīyah
AL QĀDISĪYAH
DHĪ QĀR

RDAN
An Nukhayb
An Najaf
AN NAJAF
As Samāwah
An Nāsirīyah
Al Basrah

'Ar'ar
De facto boundary as shown on official Iraqi and Saudi maps. (alignment approximate)
As Salmān
AL MUTHANNĀ
Al Busayyah
Az Zubayr
AL BASRAH
Umm Qasr

Rafhā'
Al Jahrah
Kuwa
KUWAIT
IRAQ - SAUDI ARABIA NEUTRAL ZONE

SAUDI ARABIA
As Salmān
Hafar al Bāţin
Ra's al Khaf

Iraq

International boundary
Province (muḥāfaẓah) boundary
★ National capital
◎ Province (muḥāfaẓah) capital
Railroad
Road

0   50   100 Kilometers
0   50   100 Miles
Lambert Conformal Conic Projection, SP 12N/38N

IRAQ FACTS AT A GLANCE

Country Name: Republic of Iraq
   (*Al-Jumhuriyah al-Iraqiyah*)
Capital City: Baghdad
Provinces/Governorates: 18
Land Area: 169,234 square miles (438,317 square kilometers), about the
   size of California
Highest Point: Unnamed peak, 11,847 feet (3,611 meters)
Lowest Point: Sea level, at the Persian Gulf
Population: 30,399,572 (July 2011 estimate)
Ethnic Groups: Arab (75 percent), Kurd (20 percent), minorities such as
   Assyrian, Turkoman, and Armenian (less than 5 percent)
Languages: Arabic, Kurdish
Government: Parliamentary democracy (founded October 15, 2005)
Currency: Iraqi dinar
Agricultural products: Tomatoes, buffalo milk, dates, grapes, poultry,
   sheep, cattle, wheat, eggplants
Major exports: Oil, natural gas, coal, minerals, agricultural products
   (especially tomatoes, dates, and meat)
Major imports: Food, medicine, manufactured goods
National anthem: *"Mawtini"* ("My Homeland")
Flag: Adopted January 22, 2008, as the flag of the transitional
   government, the flag has three horizontal bands of red, white, and
   black. The national motto "Allahu Akbar" (Arabic for "God Is Great")
   is inscribed on the white band in green in an ancient style of Arabic
   calligraphy that originated in
   Iraq.
National flower: Rose (*Rosa*)
National Bird: Chukar (*Alectoris chukar*)

Sources: CIA: *The World Factbook,* "Iraq," https://
www.cia.gov/library/publications/the-world-factbook/
geos/iz.html; Central Organization for Statistics and
Information Technology: "Population of Iraq," http://
cosit.gov.iq/english/AAS2010/section_2/2-1.htm; Food
and Agriculture Organization of the United Nations,
"Top Production—Iraq—2008," http://faostat.fao.org/
DesktopDefault.aspx?PageID=339&lang=en&country=103

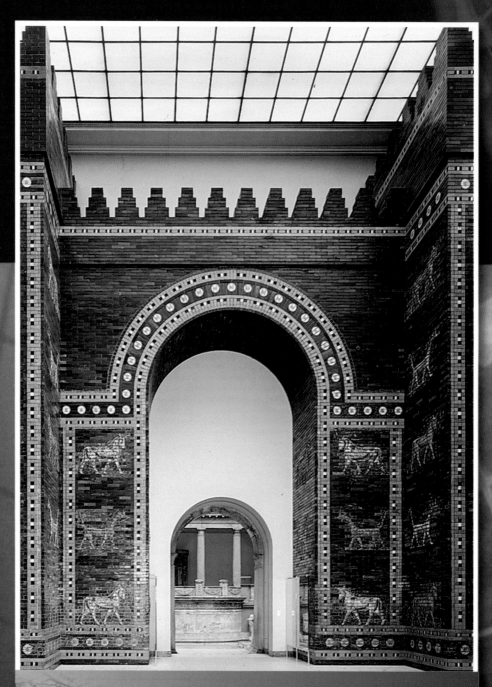

The beautiful, blue-tiled Ishtar Gate guarded the inner city of Babylon. Archaeologist Robert Koldewey (1855–1925) excavated the gate and brought it back to his hometown of Berlin, Germany, where today it is on display at the Pergamon Museum.

The Cradle of Civilization

Around 8000 BCE, people in Mesopotamia traded their lives as wandering nomads for the settled lives of farmers. Their decision revolutionized the world. Farming offers vital advantages over hunting animals and gathering wild plants to eat, such as increased safety and a guaranteed food supply. Tied to the land, people found that they could work together to improve their farms, trade goods and services with neighbors, and have fun together during their newfound free time. The first cities and governments were born in this cradle of civilization.

The world's first civilization, Sumer, arose around 3500 BCE. Sumer was not a country, but rather a network of cities that traded with one another. Sumerians invented the wheel and the plow to help them farm. To keep track of business deals and crops, they invented calendars and a system of counting based on the number 60. They pioneered the world's first system of alphabet writing, called cuneiform. Cuneiform uses 600 signs, each of which stands for a word or idea. Its usefulness caught on quickly, so Sumerians also invented schools where the children of wealthy merchants could be trained as scribes.

To keep their gods happy, Sumerians built huge, stepped temples called ziggurats out of the same mud and clay bricks they used to build their houses. Each ziggurat served as a center for religious ceremonies and sacrifices to the gods, and gave jobs to musicians, artists, poets, and storytellers. By 2011, archaeologists had discovered more than

The Ziggurat of Ur stands as a testament to the Sumerian culture. It was completed by King Shulgi of Urim, the son of Ur-Nammu, around 2100 BCE. This mud-brick temple to the sun and moon has been restored throughout history, notably by Babylonian King Nabonidus and by Saddam Hussein.

25 ziggurats, most in Iraq and Iran. The best preserved of these, the Ziggurat of Ur, dates from the 2000s BCE and still stands near the city of Nasiriyah.

The nearby nomadic Akkadians conquered Sumer in 2500 BCE. While Sumer had been content to nestle between the rivers, Akkadians expanded the territory north to the Mediterranean Sea and south to the Persian Gulf. Babylonians, led by King Hammurabi, moved in to conquer the area around 1800 BCE. Before Hammurabi died in 1750 BCE, he commanded cuneiform scribes to record 282 of his legal decisions on black stone slabs. The Code of Hammurabi still exists; it is on display at the Louvre Museum in Paris. While strict and violent—possibly the earliest written record of "an eye for an eye"—the code shows that the Babylonians used laws to promote justice and to stand up for the weak.

The ruthless and war-loving Assyrians in the north rose to great power beginning in the twelfth

Code of Hammurabi

century BCE. Their enormous 100,000-man army was the first to use durable iron weapons, destroying armies that relied on bronze ones. The Assyrians brought all of what are now Iraq, Iran, Syria, Israel, Jordan, and parts of Egypt under control of their organized government, which was headed by a warrior king. Today, the Assyrian capital city of Assur in northern Iraq is a UNESCO World Heritage Site.

The Assyrian Empire collapsed suddenly in 612 BCE, conquered by the Medes and the Chaldeans. The Chaldeans made Babylon their capital and spared no expense building it into a city of wonders. They built high walls around Babylon that could be accessed by eight elaborately decorated gates, including the stunning Ishtar Gate, covered with blue glazed tile. Legend has it that King Nebuchadnezzar II built the Hanging Gardens of Babylon—one of the Seven Wonders of the Ancient World—for his wife Amytis, a Median princess who missed the lush green of her homeland.

Exhausted, overtaxed, and abused from so many building projects, the Babylonian people welcomed the kind Persian King Cyrus when he took the city for his own in 539 BCE. For the next thousand years,

The Hanging Gardens of Babylon and the Tower of Babel (background) are mentioned in ancient literature. Neither has survived to modern times, so artists can only imagine how they looked.

many kingdoms fought for control of the kingdom of Babylon, including Macedonia, Parthia, and Rome.

Armies of Islamic warriors blew in from the deserts of Saudi Arabia to take Mesopotamia in 637 CE. The caliph Abbas fashioned Babylon into his new capital in 762, beginning the Golden Age of Islam. The Muslims called it their City of Peace, crafting the city in a perfect circle atop Babylon's ruins. The new city was named Baghdad, Persian for "God-given." The capital quickly became a world center for religion, science, art, and culture.

Wild, nomadic Mongols snuffed out the light of the Islamic Empire in 1258. Hulagu Khan, grandson of Genghis Khan, conquered Mesopotamia, destroying public buildings and irrigation canals and mercilessly killing thousands. The Mongols had no use for cities or farms. They sought to spread their lifestyle as hunter-gatherers from the untamed steppes of central Asia. Civilization in Iraq would not recover from this savage beating.

The Ottoman Turks stepped over their borders to rule Iraq in 1534. They often faced brutal opposition from the Safavid Persians in present-day Iran. The Shiite Safavids fought bitterly to expand their territory into Iraq to claim Najaf and Karbala, holy sites of martyrdom to Shiites. The Sunni Turks would not budge, determined to keep the Shiites bottled up. Over time, neither side gained or lost much territory, but vicious battles between the Turks and Safavids trained Iraqi Sunnis and Shiites to be bitter enemies.

Hulagu Khan and his queen, Dokuz

With the defeat of the Ottoman Empire in World War I, control of Iraq passed to Great Britain. Between 1920 and 1958, the British guided the Iraqi people in what appeared to be a democracy. Iraq held its first election in October 1920, where the people voted the British-chosen Prince Faisal I as their king. The British put Sunnis in government positions as the Turks had done, shutting Shiites out of government involvement until 1958. Outraged Shiites in the south revolted, only to be swiftly crushed by British forces. But Sunnis and Shiites alike detested their British "protectors." The British had no intention of giving up control of the rich oil resources discovered near Mosul in 1927. Protesters who pointed out Britain's exploitation of Iraqis and their resources were either captured and tortured, or slaughtered in the streets.

King Faisal II (1935–1958)

On the night of July 14, 1958, military troops led by Colonel Abdul-Salam Arif and Brigadier General Abd al-Karim Qasim snuck into the royal palace and killed the young King Faisal II, his family, and the Prime Minister. They took over Baghdad's radio station, shouting their victory slogan, "Iraq First," as Iraqis danced in the streets.[1] For the first time since ancient Sumer, Iraq was controlled by Iraqis. But quickly the Iraqis saw that the 14 July Revolution really meant "Qasim First." Qasim ruthlessly crushed any opponents and spent the country's money as he wished.

Support for the underground Ba'ath Party grew. Ba'athists felt that rich Arab governments should share wealth and land with their people. On February 8, 1963, a group of soldiers loyal to the Ba'ath Party captured Qasim in his office, put him to quick trial, and executed him. The Ba'ath Party kept an iron grip on Iraq through a series of presidents who ruled like dictators—Colonel Arif, Hasan al-Bakr, and finally al-Bakr's cousin, Saddam Hussein.[2]

President George W. Bush paid an official visit to Baghdad on June 13, 2006, to greet Iraqi Prime Minister Nuri (also spelled Nouri) al-Maliki and to lend his support for the newly formed Iraqi government.

Chapter

3

From Saddam Hussein to Democracy's Promise

Between 1979 and 2003, Saddam Hussein led Iraq as a totalitarian state, jailing, kidnapping, torturing, or killing anyone who dared oppose him. Books, newspapers, TV, radio, and even art were forbidden—under threat of the author's or artist's death—if the work criticized Saddam. Doctors, teachers, lawyers, and manufacturing workers all had to join the Ba'ath Party just to get jobs and to avoid arrest by the Mukhabarat, Saddam's secret police.

The power-hungry Saddam started two major wars that bankrupted Iraq and cost the lives of hundreds of thousands of his own people. Iraq invaded Iran in 1980, after Iran's new Shiite government threatened to overthrow Saddam, a Sunni Muslim. During the eight bloody years that followed, Iran's air force bombed major cities, oil fields, and refineries, crippling the economy and killing Iraqi civilians. Meanwhile, Saddam ordered his Republican Guard to attack the Shiites in the south and the Kurds in the north, groups he accused of supporting Iran. In one such attack on March 16, 1988, Saddam's forces used poison gas to injure or kill over 10,000 Kurds in the village of Halabja. As many as 250,000 people died during the war, with an additional 375,000 injured, before a cease-fire was reached in 1988.[1]

Despite the devastation, Saddam's army invaded Kuwait in August 1990, claiming the tiny, oil-rich neighbor as Iraq's nineteenth province. Countries around the world, including nations in the Arab League, demanded Iraq's immediate withdrawal. Saddam refused to obey. The United States and its United Nations (UN) allies initiated Operation

Desert Storm on January 17, 1991, driving Saddam's overwhelmed forces to surrender and retreat on February 28.

The UN demanded to see Saddam's weapons facilities as part of the cease-fire agreement reached in 1991. Saddam continually refused, even in the face of punishing sanctions that stopped trade between Iraq and the world. In 1995 the UN instituted the Oil-for-Food Programme, which allowed the sale of a limited amount of Iraqi oil. The UN controlled the profits, using the money to bring much-needed food and medicine to the Iraqi people. Meanwhile, however, Saddam continued to sell most of the country's oil on the black market. His uncooperative attitude convinced U.S. President George W. Bush that he must have had dangerous biological or even nuclear weapons to hide. Bush's armies invaded Iraq in March 2003 to find those weapons of mass destruction (WMDs). Forces led by the United States and Great Britain quickly took Baghdad on April 9, 2003, chasing Saddam and his of-ficials into hiding. U.S. forces searched in vain for the WMDs. Eight years later, they still had not been found.

Most Iraqis rejoiced at the fall of their oppressive leader. They also hoped that the United States would bring a new era of freedom and opportunity for all Iraqis. But Iraqis and their new Coalition Provisional Authority (CPA), headed by U.S. diplomats, faced a tough road paved with poor decisions. With the government in shambles, people in Iraq lost basic services they were used to having under Saddam's rule, in-cluding law enforcement, electricity, and running water. Desperate, people relied on neighborhood religious gangs to keep them safe from widespread looting and murder.

The CPA stayed holed up in the Green Zone, a protected area they created around Saddam's luxurious presidential palaces. Ignoring the everyday problems faced by all Iraqis, their task was to create a new government. In October 2005, the CPA presented a constitution to the Iraqi people, who rushed to the polls to approve it. Nearly 80 percent of Iraqis voted again in December 2005, this time to choose the 275 members of their new lawmaking body, the Council of Representatives. Ibrahim al-Jaafari was elected as the first prime minister; then Nuri al-Maliki got enough votes to unseat him in May 2006. Al-Maliki's cabinet was approved by the Council of Representatives that month, signaling that Iraq had formed its first independent, constitutional democracy. By 2008, as the new government began to provide basic services for its people, including training an Iraqi police force to replace U.S. soldiers, Iraq saw robberies and killings decline.

Iraqis continue to flock to the polls on election days. They elected provincial leaders on January 31, 2009, and voted for representatives a second time on March 7, 2010. Though votes had so far been split along ethnic lines, politicians were learning to work together. In a move hailed worldwide as an important first step, President al-Maliki formed a new cabinet that included members from Iraq's many ethnic and religious groups, including women. His cabinet choices were approved by Iraq's expanded 325-member parliament on December 21, 2010. On January 8, 2011, the popular Shiite religious leader Moktada al-Sadr spoke in favor of al-Maliki's government to thousands of supporters on the streets of Najaf. He and other Iraqis were encouraged when the last U.S. combat troops left the country on August 19, 2010, though he echoed common feelings that all peacekeeping foreign troops must keep their promise to leave by 2012.[2] If Iraq's new government can step up to provide basic services for all its people—clean water, working sewers, reliable electricity, and improved safety against terrorist attacks—then the future for Iraq may indeed be bright.

Four 30-foot-tall busts of Saddam once peered down from the roof of Al-Salam Palace in Baghdad. After the U.S. invasion in 2003, the busts were removed, and the palace was renamed Forward Operating Base Prosperity and housed American soldiers.

Shanidar Cave in the Zagros Mountains of southern Kurdistan was home to a Neanderthal tribe as early as 80,000 years ago. Neanderthal hunter-gatherers roamed Europe and eastern Asia between 100,000 and 25,000 years ago.

Chapter 4

A Land of Contrast

The Republic of Iraq (Al Jumhuriyah al-Iraqiyah) sits in the center of the Middle East, perched atop the Arabian Peninsula. This compact country, in area slightly larger than California, is nearly landlocked except for a tiny, 35-mile (58-kilometer) coastline along the Persian Gulf in the southeast. Like a dam keeping Iraq from a greater share of the Gulf, tiny Kuwait forms Iraq's southeastern border. Deserts stretch over the country's border with Saudi Arabia to the south, and continue north through the western borders with Jordan and Syria. The Taurus Mountains create a rugged, natural border between Iraq and Turkey in the north. The Zagros Mountain range in the north and the Shatt al-Arab waterway in the south form natural barriers between Iraq and Iran to the east.

Iraq's northern highlands make up about 20 percent of the land, where the Taurus Mountains meet the Zagros. Rugged, rocky peaks rise 8,000 to 11,000 feet (2,440 to 3,350 meters), separated by basins and gorges cut by ancient rivers. Iraq's highest point—an unnamed peak 11,847 feet (3,611 meters) high—looms in the country's northeast corner. The mountains coax rainfall out of passing winds, allowing farmers to grow grains—especially barley, wheat, and rice—and cotton. The area was once famous for its cotton. The light cotton cloth called muslin gets its name from the northern city of Mosul. The highlands claim the only remaining forests in Iraq, though in recent years forests have shrunk as people chop down wood for fuel.

The highlands slope downward to the southwest into the uplands of central Iraq. The land north of Samarra on the Tigris and north of Hit on the Euphrates forms a dry plateau known by locals as al-Jazirah, or "the island." Mostly desert, al-Jazirah's little rainfall is channeled by wadis, dry riverbeds carved out by flash floods. Al-Jazirah's main wadi, Wadi Tharthar, carves a winding path from Jabal Sinjar, a 4,800-foot (1,463-meter) peak near the Syrian border. Damming Wadi Tharthar created Iraq's largest lake, Lake Tharthar, which collects the wadi's precious water during the rainy season.[1]

A river-fed plain in central and southeastern Iraq makes up about a third of Iraq's land. The rich plain is home to most of Iraq's population and major cities, including the capital city, Baghdad. The Tigris and Euphrates Rivers feed this soil, the country's main sources of freshwater. Both rivers begin high in the Zagros Mountains of Turkey and flow southeast, cutting almost parallel, diagonal lines across the center of Iraq. The Euphrates is longer—1,460 miles (2,350 kilometers) versus the Tigris's 1,150 miles (1,850 kilometers)—but the Tigris carries more water, replenished by mountain streams in its northern course. Annual floods in March through May bring freshwater and nutrients

FYI FACT: Iraq experiences two seasonal winds. The *shamal*, a northwestern wind that comes mainly in the summer, brings cool winds and lasts from 3 to 5 days. The shorter but fierce *sharqi* comes from the southeast when seasons change, bringing dry and dusty air in gusts of 50 miles per hour (80 kilometers per hour). Each of these winds kicks up sandstorms several times throughout the year, ferocious enough to ground boats and airplanes and to sandblast the paint off cars.

An intricate system of canals and waterways snakes through Basra. The river water brings much-needed irrigation to nearby farms and provides an easy way to get around town.

to the soil. Civilizations there have controlled the floodwaters with dams and canals since the invention of farming. Today, Iraqis also harness the rivers' power to generate electricity with hydroelectric dams. The central plain is also home to Iraq's capital, Baghdad.

Iraq's southeast was once a natural marsh, fed by the union of the Tigris and Euphrates. The mighty rivers join near the city of al-Qurnah to form the Shatt al-Arab, which runs 100 miles (160 kilometers) along the Iraq-Iran border to empty into the Persian Gulf. The Shatt al-Arab is Iraq's only major access to shipping for import or export. Basra, the country's only major port, lies along the Shattal al-Arab 34 miles (55 kilometers) inland from the Persian Gulf. In 1992, the Iraqi government built the Main Outfall Drain—a 350-mile- (563-kilometer-) long artificial river—to move water from Iraq's marshy lowlands into irrigation canals for farming. Today, less than 15 percent of Iraq's natural marshes remain.[2] Waterbirds such as ducks, herons, and flamingoes still find homes there.

Deserts claim Iraq's southwest, from the rocky Arabian Desert in the south to the high plateau of the Syrian Desert in the west. In the southeast, the desert of Al-Dibdiba gets occasional spring rains and blooms with spear grass, rock roses, and salt bushes.

An Iraqi Bedouin woman prepares bread in her family tent in the desert of southern Iraq. This simple food will be baked over a coal fire and enjoyed with every meal.

To Be an Iraqi

Nearly three-quarters of the 30 million Iraqis consider themselves as Arabs, descended from tribes that have lived in the Middle East for thousands of years. Two minority groups of Arabs include the Marsh Arabs and the Bedouins. The Bedouins wander the deserts as family tribes, herding animals from one grazing spot to the next. Traditionally, the Bedouins have roamed throughout southern Iraq, Kuwait, and Saudi Arabia. Today, modern closed borders and the lure of big city jobs and conveniences make the traditional Bedouin life increasingly rare.

The Marsh Arabs, or Ma'dan, have called the marshlands of southern Iraq home for over 6,000 years. These unique people live as fishermen, building what they need—canoes, houses, even artificial islands—from mud and reeds. In 1992, the Marsh Arabs opposed Saddam's attack of Kuwait. Saddam drained their marshes dry, forcing over 100,000 of them to give up their homes and their ancient way of life. By 2011, less than 85 percent of the marshlands remained. Some Ma'dan, together with international human rights groups, were pleading with the new Iraqi government to reflood the marshes and restore their ancient home.

The Kurds (Persian for "heroes") hail from the mountainous, chilly north, making up about 20 percent of Iraqis. The 30 million ethnic Kurds throughout Asia occupy Kurdistan, a region encompassing parts of Iraq, Iran, Turkey, Syria, and Azerbaijan. Kurds share a language, lifestyle, and attitude because of their rugged home, but they belong to diverse religious and cultural backgrounds. On March 11, 1974, the

An Iraqi Ma'dan family builds a house out of reeds and mud gathered from the Euphrates River. Traditional building methods are making a comeback in the marshes, providing resourceful and inexpensive ways to build homes for Iraq's many refugees.

Iraqi government agreed to form a special state in the north called the Kurdish Autonomous Region (KAR), where Kurds make their own laws and maintain their own army.

Because of the nearly constant conflict in the region since 1948, Iraqis of all heritages have been driven from their homes, with an estimated 4 million people fleeing for safer parts of Iraq or even leaving the country.[1] The nearby countries of Syria and Jordan have large populations of Iraqi refugees. The World Bank estimates that, as of March 2009, less than 20 percent of Iraqis had returned, though numbers were increasing as confidence in the new government grew.[2]

Iraqis who have stayed have chosen to live mostly in large, sprawling cities like Baghdad (5.7 million), Mosul (1.4 million), Erbil (1 million), and Basra (923,000).[3] Iraq's cities have been difficult to control since the overthrow of Saddam. Suffering from patchy electrical service, unclean water, stagnant sewers, and no police to protect them, city dwellers returned to the ancient way of government—the tribe. Neighborhoods formed religious militias to protect themselves. They argue, sometimes at gunpoint, for basic services. At the peak of violence from 2006 to 2008, urban Iraqis lived in fear of car bombs or getting caught in the crossfire between rival militias.

By 2011, urban Iraqis were cautiously optimistic as the new government's police presence allowed them to return to a normal life. Diverse, progressive Baghdadis go to cafés daily to snack and drink coffee, listen to music, discuss politics, or simply meet their friends. Families especially love to go out for ice cream in the evenings of hot summer months. In beautiful but conservative Basra, families enjoy trips to the park or walks along the Shatt al-Arab waterway. The shadow of violence still hangs over northern Mosul. A teenager known as IraqiGirl has been blogging about her life in Mosul since 2004, telling the world about open violence in the streets, and how for days on end it was unsafe for her to go to school, let alone leave her house.[4]

In contrast, rural areas have seen little action. Rural tribes, formed from local families, do not rely on the national government to maintain day-to-day order. They prefer instead to work locally to make and act on decisions that improve their villages, as they have done for centuries. The tight-knit communities keep the peace using only stern words to shame those who would join violent militia groups.

As of 2009, the average life expectancy of an Iraqi was 68 to 72 years for females, 64 years for males.[5] By comparison, Israel boasts the region's oldest residents, with an average life expectancy of 80 years. Iraq's population is also very young, with 41 percent of its population 14 years old or younger. With the average Iraqi woman bearing more than 4 children in her lifetime, experts expect the population to double by 2030. A population boom brings fresh worries for the new Iraqi government. How will the next generation find jobs, when in this generation one in five workers is unemployed?

An Iraqi worker adjusts a control valve at the Daura oil refinery in Baghdad, Iraq. Iraq's current oil production is far below its potential, making the oil sector attractive to foreign investors. The government hopes that developing Iraqi oil production will heal its war-ravaged economy.

Chapter 6

Resources and Jobs

Though farms have grown Iraq's past, oil certainly fuels its present and future. On October 15, 1927, the British-owned Turkish Petroleum Company discovered oil deposits near Kirkuk. The British kept tight control of Iraq's oil industry, making deals with foreign companies and giving almost none of the profits to Iraqis. Great Britain's unfair business dealings drove the Iraqis to take back their government by violence in the 14 July Revolution in 1958.

Once in power, Iraqi dictators continued to do business with foreigners. The Ba'ath Party revolutionized Iraq's oil industry by nationalizing it, kicking oil corporations out of Iraq in 1973 and running the entire oil industry through the government. Nationalization made profits soar, with production at its greatest in 1979 at 3.5 million barrels a day. After that, Iraq's oil industry suffered heavily from Saddam's wars, when employees changed into soldier uniforms and enemy bombs targeted oil fields and pipelines.

Iraq belongs to the Organization of the Petroleum Exporting Countries (OPEC) cartel, which regulates 40 percent of the world's oil supply and trade. OPEC gives Iraq free rein to produce all they can to help the country build back its economy and recover from the destruction of oil facilities by wars and Saddam Hussein's government. By 2011, the country was producing about 2.5 million barrels of oil per day—less than in previous years but still enough to fund 80 percent of its economy. Engineers estimated that over 143,000 billion barrels of oil lay beneath Iraq's soil.[1] Its proven reserves are the second-largest in the world. Iraq's largest oil fields lie under the cities of Mosul and Kirkuk, in territory often disputed with the Kurds.

Iraq boasts many other natural resources. Natural gas deposits are often found side by side with petroleum. Minerals mined and exported include coal from the Zagros Mountains, sulfur deposits near Mosul, and phosphate in the Syrian Desert. Limestone from the uplands and highlands is used throughout the region to make building materials, cement, and gypsum. Manufacturing industries, expanded greatly under Saddam, include oil refining, food processing, and textiles.

Iraq's twin rivers provide the country with a steady supply of water, fish, and farmland, rare resources in the deserts of the Middle East. Iraq's farms supply about 21 percent of the country's gross domestic product, along with the majority of jobs in rural Iraq.[2] Iraqi farmers use the fertile land to grow wheat, barley, rice, vegetables, dates, and cotton, and to raise cattle, sheep, and poultry. But the rivers that have watered the Middle East's breadbasket carry extra salt with them. Poorly constructed irrigation canals and ditches leave behind mineral deposits that poison the earth for plant growth, making less land available for crops every year. In the southeast, Iraqis now farm the salt. Large salt mining and processing factories line the Bahr al Milh, or Salt Sea, located 12 miles (20 kilometers) southwest of Samawah.

Despite its great potential, the Iraqi economy is weak. The average Iraqi worker earns $3,600 per year.[3] In the Middle East, only Yemenis

Chicken farm in Zambraniyah, Iraq

A farmer and his son in Ramaana, Iraq, prepare crops for shipment and sale. Though agriculture has long been important to Iraq's economy, Iraqi farmers struggle to recover from years of war.

are poorer. The government estimates that 20 percent of Iraqis are unemployed, though that number may be much higher, especially among young adults and women.

Perhaps the biggest obstacle facing Iraq's economy is one that most of us take for granted. The patchy electricity supply in the aftermath of the 2003 invasion has devastated businesses, especially in major cities. Without electricity to power factories, businesses must close their doors and move out of the country, taking precious jobs with them. Neither can Iraqis work from home. Some Baghdad residents report that on lucky days they get only one uninterrupted hour of power. Most people share gasoline-powered generators, which are expensive and not powerful enough to make a refrigerator work. Less than one percent of Iraqis have access to the Internet,[4] mostly because they cannot power computers. Summers without air conditioning can be a health hazard, especially in southern cities. The lack of electricity is a major source of frustration for the modern, progressive Iraqi people. As the Arab world rioted against their corrupt governments in spring 2011, Iraq's citizens urged their new government to bring them a steady supply of electricity, and with it, the jobs they desperately needed.

Forty days after Ashura, Shiites observe Arbae'en, mourning the death of the Prophet Muhammad's grandson Hussein. Large gatherings and public events on Shiite holidays were forbidden under Saddam's reign. Since his overthrow in 2003, throngs of pilgrims can travel to Hussein's tomb at Karbala.

Chapter

7

Allahu Akbar,
God Is Great

Life in Iraq is tied to Islam, the country's official state religion. Nearly all Iraqis—over 97 percent—are Muslim. It is hard to understand life in Iraq without understanding the religion of Islam.

Worldwide, Islam is divided into two major sects. Sunni Muslims make up 80 to 90 percent of world Muslims, but only 32 to 37 percent of Iraq's Islamic population. Sunnis live in Iraq's cities, their population concentrated in a central triangle between the cities of Baghdad, Tikrit, and Fallujah.[1] They believe that any faithful, learned Muslim can serve as an imam, or spiritual leader. Shi'a Islam disagrees, insisting that leaders be descended from the Prophet Muhammad. Though this point may seem small to outsiders, disagreement between Sunnis and Shiites has resulted in bitter violence since the death of Muhammad in 632 CE.

Though Shiites number only 10 to 20 percent of Muslims worldwide, their numbers are concentrated in Iraq and Iran. Shiites make up a large majority (65 percent) of Iraq's Muslim population and live primarily in rural areas. They also live in cities of southeastern Iraq near the two holiest sites in Shiite Islam, the golden-domed Shrine of Ali in Najaf and the Tomb of Hussein in Karbala. Shi'a, whose name is short for "party of Ali," believe that Muhammad's cousin Ali held Allah's favor and should have been caliph after Muhammad. Instead, Ali served as the fourth caliph, but he was assassinated by one of his generals in 661. Ali's son Hussein tried to overthrow the new government and install himself as the caliph. In 680, he rallied supporters to

37

fight for his cause and staged a great battle near Karbala. When the supporters never showed up, Hussein and his troops were slaughtered. Shiites believe Hussein was a martyr, betrayed by Muslims everywhere. His tomb in Karbala is so revered by Shiites that many rest their heads on a piece of clay from the site when they pray.

Whether Shiite or Sunni, Islam guides every Iraqi in several ways. Laws in many Arab countries, including Iraq, are heavily influenced by *shari'a,* or Islamic law, especially in matters of marriage and divorce. Islam's *sunnah,* or ways of living, are spelled out in the holy book of the Koran and in the Hadith, accounts of Muhammad's life and deeds. The *sunnah* command Muslims to help the poor. During riots throughout the Arab world in the spring of 2011, Iraqis applauded their prime minister Nuri al-Maliki when he canceled an order of fighter planes from the United States, using the money instead to feed Iraq's poor and jobless. The *sunnah* also command Muslims to dress and act modestly. Iraqi men prefer to wear a *thawb,* a loose, long-sleeved robe, over light pants called *serwal* throughout the year. Women choose loose, flowing long-sleeved dresses, with a separate scarf to cover their hair. Though not required by law as in other Islamic countries, some women wear the full-length, flowing black gown, or burka, that covers everything but their eyes. In all things, the *sunnah* urge Muslims to be honest and fair. Iraqis strained against the corrupt governments of dictators like Saddam Hussein, and they continue to protest against the new democratic government when they disagree with its actions.

Iraqis observe Islam's holidays, which follow the lunar calendar. During the holy month of Ramadan, Muslims do not eat or drink from dawn until dusk to remember how Muhammad received the words of the Koran from Allah. A special drum calls Iraqis each morning just before dawn to start their day with a special meal, called *suhur.* At dusk, a cannon fires to signal the end of the day's fast. Traditional families eat a date first, as the Prophet did, and then share *iftar,* a meal of soup

FYI FACT:

Less than 3 percent of Iraqis are Christian. Iraq's two largest Christian groups are the Assyrians, descendants from the ancient warring tribe of the northeast, and the Armenians, who live in Iraq as refugees.[2]

Iraqi Kurds celebrate Norwuz, the Persian New Year. Kurds welcome the first day of spring with this important festival of music and dancing. The most daring men jump over a fire to ward off bad luck.

served with milk. Ramadan ends with Eid al-Fitr, a three-day celebration full of parties and feasting. To symbolize a new beginning, families clean the house and give children new clothes. Many couples marry during Eid al-Fitr.

Eid al-Adha is a four-day festival honoring Ibrahim (the Bible's Abraham) for obeying God's word, even to the point of almost sacrificing his son Ishmael (or, in the Bible, Isaac). Families who can afford it roast a whole lamb and hold a feast for family and friends, saving one-third of the meat to give to the poor.

Ashura is an annual day of mourning for Shiites, held on the 10th day of Muharram, that commemorates the death of Hussein in 680 CE. Shiites grieve together as Hussein's story of bravery and suffering at the hands of enemy Muslims is reenacted through plays and passionate readings.

Inspired by his blog about life in war-torn Baghdad, the British Broadcasting Corporation asked 30-year-old architect Salam Pax to film a series of video diaries about the Iraqi people. *Baghdad Bloggers/Salam Pax—Video Reports from Iraq* premiered at the prestigious Vancouver International Film Festival in Vancouver, British Columbia, Canada, in 2004.

Chapter 8

Language and Learning

Iraq's official language is Arabic, brought to the region by Muslims in the seventh century CE. Iraqis use three different forms of Arabic. All Arabs can speak Classical Arabic. Islam expects its faithful to recite passages from the Koran written in this ancient and holy language. Modern Standard Arabic (MSA) developed over time from its roots in the Koran. MSA is the standard written language used in the news or in books. Arabic can be further broken down into dialects, based on where the speaker is from. Iraqi Spoken Arabic sounds much like dialects spoken in Syria, Lebanon, and parts of Jordan.

Iraqis in different regions might also speak languages from their home culture. Kurdish, spoken by Iraqi Kurds, is the official language of the Kurdistan Autonomous Region. Assyrians in the north speak Syriac, an ancient Aramaic language related to the language spoken by Jesus of Nazareth. Turkoman, a Turkish dialect, can be heard from Turkish peoples or those living near the northern borders.

As the birthplace of the written word, Iraq has a rich history of language. In 2000 BCE, the Akkadians recorded the world's first written story, *The Epic of Gilgamesh,* which told of the adventures of an ancient god-like king. Scholars of Islam's Golden Age wrote *Tales from 1001 Nights* in 850 CE. This collection of folktales from Arabia, Persia, and India includes the famous stories of Sinbad the Sailor and Ali Baba. In modern times, Iraqis wrote some of the first world-famous blogs, or Internet diaries. Writers such as Baghdad's Salam Pax and Mosul's

IraqiGirl showed outsiders what life was like in Iraq during the U.S. invasion and occupation—a strange world where ordinary, sophisticated, educated Iraqis risked their lives just by going out for ice cream.

Words—either written or spoken—suffered from censorship under Saddam. Reporters, poets, or authors who spoke out against him could be jailed or killed. Some left the country permanently, including internationally famous Basra-born poet Saadi Youssef. The news industry exploded when Saddam's heavy hand was lifted in 2003. By 2011, more than 20 newspapers and a dozen TV stations were operating in freedom.

Iraqis got their first taste of independent talk radio when Radio *Diljah* (Arabic for "Radio Tigris") began broadcasting in 2004. Aswat al-Iraq (Voice of Iraq) was the first independent news agency established after the overthrow of Saddam Hussein. Newspapers throughout the world use Aswat reports on Iraqi events and issues, and its journalists have won international awards for their work. The most popular Iraqi-printed newspaper is *Azzaman,* a fair and unbiased daily distributed across Iraq and available online in Arabic and English. Nearly 40 percent of Iraqis tune their television sets to Al-Iraqiya, while Kurds prefer to get their news from Ishtar TV, headquartered in Erbil. Al-Sharqiya TV features entertainment programs, including Iraq's first reality TV shows.

Literacy is a point of national pride in Iraq, and was actually a passion of Saddam Hussein's. His government required elementary school children to attend school, and offered free education to anyone up through high school. Adults who would not learn how to read faced jail time. Saddam's efforts resulted in a 90 percent literacy rate, unheard of at the time for Middle Eastern countries.

Thirty years of warfare unraveled Saddam's progress. As the country rebuilt following his overthrow, children crowded into dirty schools in need of repair, eager to learn from under-trained teachers. Just getting to school could literally be a battle in areas where violence still raged in the street. In 2009, elementary school dropouts rose to an average of 15 percent, 30 percent among rural schoolgirls.[1] That year, Iraq's literacy rate among adults fell to 78 percent.[2] Its new government

In Taji, Iraq, Iraqi girls celebrate the opening day of their new school on October 12, 2009. The "Twin Schools" would educate over 1,200 girls and boys in this small village north of Baghdad.

proposed to increase education spending to make Iraqi schools a source of pride once more.

Iraq's universities are beginning to return to their former glory. The newly formed Iraqi Ministry of Higher Education and Scientific Research (MOHESR) oversees nearly 40 public and private universities throughout the country[3] and hopes to bring a new Golden Age of learning to Iraq. One of the MOHESR's goals is to convince professors who fled the country in the face of death threats and bombings from militant Islamists to return. By 2011, over 80,000 students were attending the University of Baghdad, making it one of the largest universities in the Middle East.

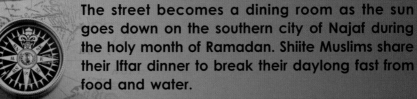

The street becomes a dining room as the sun goes down on the southern city of Najaf during the holy month of Ramadan. Shiite Muslims share their Iftar dinner to break their daylong fast from food and water.

Family, Food, and Fun

An old Arab saying goes, "My brother and I against my cousin, my cousin and I against the stranger." Above all, Iraqis are family people. Many Iraqis live with several generations under one roof, even before violence and poverty forced older and younger generations to stay together. When a girl marries, she leaves her house to live with her husband's family. Sons are considered special blessings because they remain with the family, remembering the family's traditions and heritage while adding their own wealth and children.

According to Islamic tradition, the oldest male in the house is the family leader. His word is final on important family decisions such as property, money, and the children. His influence extends even to the adult children in the household. He may decide for them what career to take or whom to marry. Though strict, his decisions consider the needs of the whole family. Acting thoughtfully is important in a society where mistakes by one family member bring shame on the entire house.

Throughout the Middle East, Iraq has a reputation for having some of the most flavorful cuisine, perhaps because more fruits and vegetables grow there than in neighboring countries. Iraq is particularly famous for its dates, which thrive in the floodwaters of the Tigris and Euphrates rivers. City-dwelling Iraqis buy their food like their ancient ancestors did—at open-air markets, or souks. A typical Iraqi breakfast includes eggs, cheese drizzled with *dibis* (date syrup), pita bread, and milk. Lunch often brings thick stews, especially of lamb or chickpeas and vegetables, served over rice or bread. Dinner favorites include shish

A contractor, Ali Jadaan, invited troops of the Oregon Army National Guard into his home for a feast just before Ramadan. Jadaan's family in Scania, Iraq, prepared fresh and pickled fruits and vegetables, fresh-baked flatbread, soup, and a hearty chicken stew over rice for their guests.

kebabs—roasted chunks of lamb skewered on a stick—and stuffed eggplant and peppers. Dessert usually consists of fruit or pastries filled with almonds and dates. Hospitality is very important to Iraqis. Even if the family has little to offer, a host must make sure his guest is served first.

Traditional folk music in Iraq reflects the country's Arab, Persian, and Turkish heritage. Violins, drums, and the *oud*—an ancient, pear-shaped Arabian lute—accompany high-pitched singing. Iraqi *oud* master Munir Bashir (1930–1997) introduced the modern classical music world to the haunting beauty of Arabian music styles.

Master *oud* player Rahim Al-Haj delights audiences the world over with his concerts and Grammy-nominated recordings. Al-Haj fled to the United States in 2000 to escape persecution from Saddam's regime. He became a U.S. citizen in 2008 and lives in New Mexico.

Iraqis enjoy western-style music as well. The Iraqi National Symphony Orchestra, based in Baghdad since 1944, performs Western and Arabian classical pieces for audiences worldwide. Streaming across Baghdad's radio waves is a mix of Arabian and Western pop music on Iraq's most popular radio station, Voice of Youth. Pop star Kadim Al Saher, born in Mosul in 1957, sings romantic ballads, political songs, and classical pieces in his native Arabic language. With over 30 million records sold, this "Elvis of the Middle East" serves as an unofficial ambassador of the Iraqi people.

The Kids Day Festival in Kirkuk, held annually on June 1, celebrates the city's history and heritage with costumes, music, rides, and family fun.

Like much of the world, Iraqis adore soccer. They take great pride in their national soccer team, the green-and-white Lions of Mesopotamia. Iraq's underdog team inspired its people when they finished fourth in the 2004 Olympic Games, and then brought home the Asian Football Confederation Cup in 2007. Iraq is also home to several nationally famous athletes. Baghdad-born Riyadh al-Azzawi took the World Kickboxing Network title in 2008. Fellow Baghdadi Adnan Al-Kaissie, also known as General Adnan, wrestled in the U.S. World Wrestling Federation in the 1990s.

IRAQI DINNER PARTY: Your Iraqi friend invited you to dinner! When you enter the house, everyone rises to greet you. You greet people of your gender only, shaking their hand and kissing them on both cheeks, saying *"Salaam Alaikum."* This common Arabic greeting means "peace be upon you." The children of the house run to see who has come. Be sure to have small gifts for them, like stickers or crayons.

You are shown to the best room in the house, where your host offers coffee or tea to drink. You take it, sipping politely. When dinner is ready, you gather with your hosts at a low table. Everyone passes a bowl of thick, steaming lamb-and-vegetable stew called *bamiyan* that you spoon into your bowl, covering a warm piece of fresh-baked flatbread called *tanour.* The sweet spicy scent of cardamom warms you as you eat the stew, right down to the broth-soaked *tanour.* Your hostess insists—an empty bowl means you need seconds. The spicy stew makes you thirsty, but you must wait your turn for the common water glass. When it comes to your place, you fill it, drink it, and pass it to the next person.

For dessert, your hostess offers fresh watermelon and sweet Iraqi dates. You go back to the parlor for more coffee and tea, and for the Iraqi national pastime—small talk! You and your hosts talk and laugh about family, friends, and life until way past everyone's bedtime.

The body of the Shiite martyr Hussein rests inside this elaborate tomb, under the dome of the Imam Hussein Shrine in Karbala. The road between Karbala and Najaf, Iraq, where Hussein's father, Ali, is buried, is well-worn by centuries' worth of Shiite pilgrims.

Chapter 10

We Visit Iraq

Travel to Iraq in ancient times would have been the experience of a lifetime, a chance to see the Hanging Gardens of Babylon or the golden-topped mosques of Baghdad. Before the Iran-Iraq War, Iraq invited tourists from France, Germany, and Japan to feast their eyes on the country's many archaeological sites and ruins, evidence of an ancient land that spread its culture and religion to much of the world. Over 1.3 million tourists visited Iraq in 2009.[1] Most of them came from Iran to pray at the Shiite holy sites of Karbala and Najaf, but a growing number were coming from the world over to experience what Iraq has to offer. Naturally, many would-be visitors will not risk their lives to experience Iraq's treasures, but as Iraq's new government grows stronger, the country's potential as the next big tourist destination does, too.

Historical treasures abound in Iraq. Starting in the north near the Turkish border is Mosul. The city boasts one of the most diverse populations in the country, where Kurds, Turkomans, historic Assyrians, and Arabs mingle. Iraq's second-largest city, located 246 miles (396 kilometers) north of Baghdad in the highlands, was first known as Nineveh, the ancient Assyrian city whose ruins lie across the Tigris River. The majestic Hatra ruins near Al-Hadar, 68 miles (110 kilometers) southwest of Mosul, date back to the second century BCE. Once a lively trading center of the Parthian Empire, Hatra's well-preserved temples celebrate the gods of Greece, Mesopotamia, Assyria, and Arabia.

51

Travel from Mosul to Erbil, 52 miles (84 kilometers) east, and pass the battlefield where Alexander the Great defeated Persian Emperor Darius III in 331 BCE. This capital of the Kurdistan Autonomous Region is also one of the oldest continually inhabited cities in the world. As early as 4000 BCE, Sumerians built an enormous citadel mound that rises 100 feet (30 meters) above the surrounding land. This mound lies at the heart of modern Erbil.

The city of Samarra lies 84 miles (135 kilometers) north of Baghdad along the Tigris. The Great Mosque of Samarra, built between 848 and 852 CE, is one of the largest in the world. Its minaret winds up to the sky in a tall spiral of sandstone. The city itself also houses the tomb of the twelfth imam, a sacred destination for Shiite Muslims worldwide.

Iraqis have a saying, "All roads lead to Baghdad," Iraq's beautiful capital along the Tigris River. Must-see sites include sculptures carved during Saddam's reign. The Monument of Martyrs—an enormous split dome, painted brilliant blue—commemorates Iraqis who died during the Iran-Iraq War. Saddam led parades under his Victory Arch, where larger-than-life swords cross 130 feet (40 meters) in the air. Baghdad also houses world treasures at the National Museum of Iraq and the National Library. A short 22-mile (35-kilometer) drive outside town lie the ruins of the elaborate stone palace Ctesiphon, once a great capital

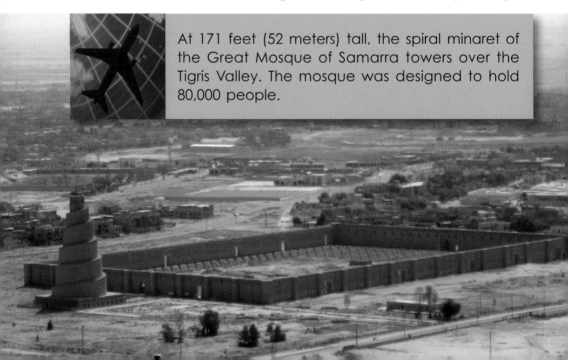

At 171 feet (52 meters) tall, the spiral minaret of the Great Mosque of Samarra towers over the Tigris Valley. The mosque was designed to hold 80,000 people.

The Victory Arch, and the Grand Festivities Square it guards, were unveiled on August 8, 1989, commissioned by Saddam to commemorate his "victory" over Iran in the Iran-Iraq War. Sculptor Adil Kamil used Saddam's hands to model the sculpture. The steel sword blades alone weigh 24 tons, made in part from the melted-down guns and tanks of Iraqi soldiers killed in the war.

of the Parthian and then Persian empire. In the sixth century CE, it was the largest city in the world.

The ancient city of Babylon, 55 miles (89 kilometers) south of Baghdad, lies in ruins. Saddam began a reconstruction program in 1985 to rebuild the great city. He spared no expense, hiring local craftsman to make bricks the old-fashioned way. The UN continues Saddam's initiative, and today Babylon's rebuilt Ishtar Gate waits to guard new walls.

Basra, a watery town built atop a system of canals, sits on the Shatt al-Arab. Its strategic location gives it a long human history. The Sumerian capital of Uruk was located near there. The modern city was founded by the Imam Omar in 637 CE and became a famous center for Islamic scholars. Iraq's only major port is also the fabled home of Sinbad the Sailor. Its distant location from Baghdad—340 miles (550 kilometers) to the northwest—often makes its residents feel more strongly tied to Shiites in Iran than to their own government, historically controlled by Sunnis.

An Iraqi market, or souk

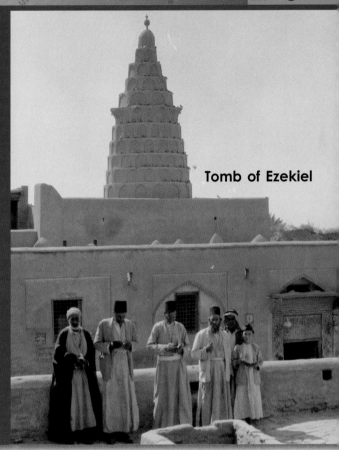

Many prophets common to Islam, Judaism, and Christianity rest in tombs in Iraq. Ezekiel, who predicted the fall of Jerusalem in the sixth century BCE, is buried at Kefil. Ezra led his people from Babylon to Jerusalem in 458 BCE; his tomb lies on the Tigris River in the village of Al-Uzair. Jonah, who became a prophet in the city of Nineveh after being swallowed by a whale, is said to be buried near Mosul. Daniel shared his visions of the future with Babylonian King Nebuchadnezzar; his body rests in the Kirkuk Citadel.

Tomb of Ezekiel

The Great Ziggurat of Ur awaits about 120 miles (193 kilometers) from Basra and 10 miles (16 kilometers) from the nearby city of Na-siriyah. Sumerian ruler Ur-Nammu had this artificial mountain built in 2100 BCE. The people of Ur believed that their moon god, Nanna, lived at the summit of the seven-story structure with his wife, Ningal. Sumerians named this ziggurat *Etemennigur,* meaning "house whose foundation creates terror."[2] Biblical and Islamic scholars also believe Ur may have been the birthplace of the prophet Abraham.

Tourism can help bring money and interest to Iraq's cultural sites, many of which have suffered from neglect and destruction during the wars of the past thirty years. As Iraq becomes more secure, the country's many amazing cultural sites can offer much to tourists seeking to be wowed by history. Certainly, visitors gain the most by meeting the Iraqi people and experiencing their laughter, conversation, and determination firsthand.

Iraqi Masgouf

In Iraq, this favorite fish dish is made with *masgouf*, a fish found in the Tigris River. Fishermen catch the fish, split it open to make it lie flat like a pancake, and cook it over a fire in a flat wooden basket. Impress your friends and family with traditional Iraqi flavors when you make this easy *masgouf*-style dish with fish you can find at your butcher's or grocery store. Please ask **an adult** for help.

Ingredients
5 pounds whole fish (such as trout or bluefish)
¼ cup vegetable oil
5 cloves garlic, crushed or minced
2 tablespoons tomato paste
½ cup lemon juice
1 teaspoon curry powder
½ teaspoon ground coriander
1 teaspoon salt
Cooking spray
1 large onion, sliced
2 large tomatoes, sliced
½ cup chopped parsley
Cooked rice

Instructions
1. When you buy the fish, ask your butcher to slice the whole fish down the middle along the spine, leaving the skin intact at the bottom of the cut.
2. At home, wash the fish and pat it dry with paper towels. Place a colander in the sink and lay the fish in the colander, skin side down. Sprinkle a small amount of salt evenly over the fish and let it drain for 30 minutes.
3. Prepare a spice mixture to season the fish. In a small bowl, combine the oil, garlic, tomato paste, lemon juice, curry powder, coriander, and salt to make a paste.
4. Preheat an oven to 400°F. Grease a rimmed jellyroll pan or cookie sheet with cooking spray. Lay the fish, skin side down, on the tray. Rub the spice paste over the meat of the fish. Arrange the sliced tomatoes and onions atop the fish and sprinkle with chopped parsley.
5. Bake the fish in the preheated oven for 30 to 35 minutes.
6. Serve with cooked rice for an authentic Iraqi meal.

Cuneiform Tablet

The ancient Sumerians invented cuneiform, the world's first writing system. They didn't have pencils and paper like we do. Instead, these river people preserved their ideas by pressing shaped stiff reeds into soft, damp river clay. When the clay dried, the reed marks—and the language they represented— were preserved forever. Many of these durable clay tablets still exist. In fact, anthropologists know more about life in ancient Sumeria than they do about Europe during the Dark Ages.

You will need
2 cups flour
1 cup salt
1 cup water
1½ tablespoons vegetable oil
Mixing bowl
spoon
Wax paper
Rolling pin
Toothpick and a small wedge shape, like the head of a golf tee or a game piece from Trivial Pursuit
Cookie sheet
Butter knife

Cuneiform alphabet
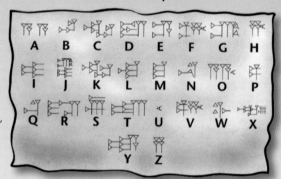

Instructions
1. Mix the flour and salt together in the mixing bowl. Stir as you slowly add the water and vegetable oil. Mix until you have a smooth, dough-like clay.
2. Turn out the clay onto a very large piece of wax paper. Roll it into a smooth, flat rectangle, about ½ inch thick.
3. Look at the chart above to determine how to spell your name in the cuneiform alphabet. Like English, cuneiform is written from left to right. Write your name out on paper a few times to practice.
4. Write the symbols in your name using proper cuneiform technique! Press the toothpick and wedge or golf tee into the clay to copy the symbols in your name as you wrote them in step 3.
5. Ancient cuneiform scribes would leave their clay tablets in the sun to dry. With the help of **an adult**, you can bake yours in the oven with the same results. Preheat an oven to 250°F. Trim your tablet to a desired size by cutting away extra clay with a butter knife. You can keep the trimmings in a sealed container for another tablet or project. Carry the cuneiform tablet on its wax paper to a cookie sheet. Bake the tablet in a preheated oven for 45 minutes to an hour, or until the project is completely dry and stiff. Set the tablet aside to cool.

TIMELINE

3500 BCE	Sumer, the world's first known civilization, develops in Mesopotamia.
2500 BCE	Sumerians are conquered by Akkadians. *Epic of Gilgamesh* is written.
c. 2100 BCE	Great Ziggurat of Ur is constructed.
1800–1750 BCE	Rule of Hammurabi; Code of Hammurabi is chiseled in stone.
1170–612 BCE	The Assyrians flourish.
612–539 BCE	Chaldeans rule Babylon.
539 BCE	Persians under Cyrus the Great conquer Mesopotamia.
331 BCE	Alexander the Great conquers Mesopotamia.
238 BCE–224 CE	The Parthians rule Mesopotamia.
224 CE	Sassanid dynasty of Persia conquers Mesopotamia.
642–1258 CE	Islamic caliphate controls all of Iraq.
900 CE	Baghdad becomes the first city in the world with over 1 million inhabitants.
1258	The Mongols invade Mesopotamia.
1534–1918	The Ottoman Empire includes Mesopotamia.
1920	The League of Nations grants Britain a mandate over Iraq.
1921	Prince Faisal bin Hussein Ali al-Hashemi is crowned king of Iraq.
1927	A supergiant oil field is discovered near Kirkuk.
1932	The League of Nations grants Iraq independence from Britain.
1958	On July 14, Brigadier Abd al-Karim Qasim leads a bloody coup to overthrow the monarchy, forming the Republic of Iraq.
1963	Qasim is ousted in a coup. Abdul Rahman Mohammed Arif Aljumaily becomes president.
1968	The nationalist, socialist Ba'ath Party takes over, with Ahmad Hasan al-Bakr as president.
1973	The Iraqi government completes the takeover of foreign oil facilities in Iraq.
1974	Kurdish Autonomous Region is established.
1979	Saddam Hussein becomes president of Iraq.
1980	On September 22, Iraq invades Iran, sparking the eight-year Iran-Iraq War.
1988	Under Saddam's cousin "Chemical Ali," Iraq uses chemical weapons to attack Kurds in Halabja in March. Thousands of people are killed.
1990	Iraq invades Kuwait on August 2.
1991	In February, forces from 39 nations defeat Iraq in the Persian Gulf War, reestablishing Kuwait's independence.
1995	On April 14, the UN establishes the Oil-for-Food Programme; it will go into operation in December 1996.
2003	U.S. begins war with a "shock and awe" bombing of Baghdad on March 20. As of May 28, some $28 billion worth of humanitarian supplies and equipment has been delivered to Iraq under the Oil-for-Food Programme, including $1.6 billion in parts and equipment for the oil industry.
2005	On October 15, a new constitution is approved by Iraqi voters, creating an Islamic democracy. Iraqis vote on a full-term government on December 15.
2006	Saddam Hussein is executed for crimes against humanity on December 30.
2009	In January, control of Baghdad's "Green Zone" is passed to the Iraqi government.
2010	Chemical Ali receives his fourth conviction for crimes against humanity. The last U.S. combat brigade leaves Iraq in August. In December, the Iraqi Parliament approves a newly elected government.
2011	Riots throughout the Arab world call for corrupt leaders to step down, including Egypt's longstanding President Hosni Mubarak. On May 1, U.S. Navy Seals kill Al-Qaeda leader Osama Bin Laden in Pakistan.

Introduction
1. Clayton R. Koppes, "Captain Mahan, General Gordon, and the Origins of the Term 'Middle East,' " *Middle Eastern Studies,* vol.12, n. 1, 1976, pp. 95–98.

Chapter 1. Iraq, Birthplace of History
1. Tertius Chandler, *Four Thousand Years of Urban Growth: An Historical Census* (Lewiston, NY: The Edwin Mellen Press, 1987), p. 312.

Chapter 2. The Cradle of Civilization
1. William R. Polk, *Understanding Iraq* (New York: HarperCollins, 2005), p. 111.
2. Ibid., p. 115.

Chapter 3. From Saddam Hussein to Democracy's Promise
1. GlobalSecurity.org, "Iran-Iraq War (1980–1988)," http://www.globalsecurity.org/military/world/war/iran-iraq.htm
2. Anthony Shadid, "Iraqi Cleric Embraces State in Comeback Speech," *The New York Times,* January 8, 2011, http://www.nytimes.com/2011/01/09/world/middleeast/09iraq.html

Chapter 4. A Land of Contrast
1. Jon C. Malinowski, *Geographic Perspectives: Iraq* (Guilford, CT: McGraw-Hill/Dushkin, 2004), p. c-5.
2. Ibid., p. 9.

Chapter 5. To Be an Iraqi
1. IraqiGirl, *IraqiGirl: Diary of a Teenage Girl in Iraq* (Chicago: Haymarket Books, 2009), p. 173.
2. The World Bank, "Iraq," June 6, 2010, http://web.worldbank.org/WBSITE/EXTERNAL/COUNTRIES/MENAEXT/IRAQEXTN/0,,menuPK:313111~pagePK:141159~piPK:141110~theSitePK:313105,00.html
3. U.S. Central Intelligence Agency, "Iraq," *The World Factbook,* February 14, 2011, https://www.cia.gov/library/publications/the-world-factbook/geos/iz.html

4. IraqiGirl, http://iraqigirl.blogspot.com/
5. The World Bank.

Chapter 6. Resources and Jobs
1. *BBC News,* "Iraq Increases Oil Reserves by 24 Percent," October 4, 2010, http://www.bbc.co.uk/news/business-11468209
2. The World Bank, "Iraq," June 6, 2010, http://web.worldbank.org/WBSITE/EXTERNAL/COUNTRIES/MENAEXT/IRAQEXTN/0,,menuPK:313111~pagePK:141159~piPK:141110~theSitePK:313105,00.html
3. U.S. Central Intelligence Agency, "Iraq," *The World Factbook,* February 14, 2011, https://www.cia.gov/library/publications/the-world-factbook/geos/iz.html
4. Internet World Stats, "Middle East Internet Usage Stats and Facebook Statistics," September 20, 2010, http://www.internetworldstats.com/middle.htm#iq

Chapter 7. *Allahu Akbar,* God Is Great
1. Melissa Rossi, *What Every American Should Know About The Middle East* (New York: Penguin Books, 2008), p. 123.
2. U.S. Central Intelligence Agency, "Iraq," *The World Factbook,* February 14, 2011, https://www.cia.gov/library/publications/the-world-factbook/geos/iz.html

Chapter 8. Language and Learning
1. Inter-Agency Information and Analysis Unit, "Education in Iraq," April 2010, http://www.iauiraq.org/reports/mdgs/Education-Factsheet-English-v2.pdf
2. The World Bank, "Iraq," June 6, 2010, http://web.worldbank.org/WBSITE/EXTERNAL/COUNTRIES/MENAEXT/IRAQEXTN/0,,menuPK:313111~pagePK:141159~piPK:141110~theSitePK:313105,00.html
3. Republic of Iraq Ministry of Higher Education and Scientific Research, http://www.mohesr.gov.iq/EngPages/indexE.htm

ISRAEL

Alexandria   Port Jerusalem   West Bank D E S E R T   I
Said   Amman
Dead Sea
(lowest point in Asia, -408 m)
Cairo   Suez Canal   Gaza Strip   JORDAN

Chapter 10. We Visit Iraq

1. World Travel Market, "Iraq, the Next Tourism Hot Spot," November 8, 2010, http://www.wtmlondon.com/page.cfm/T=m/Action=Press/PressID=1755

2. The British Museum, "Ziggurats," http://www.mesopotamia.co.uk/ziggurats/index.html

FURTHER READING

Books

Fast, April. *Iraq the Culture*. New York: Crabtree Publishing Company, 2010.
———. *Iraq the Land*. New York: Crabtree Publishing Company, 2010.
———. *Iraq the People*. New York: Crabtree Publishing Company, 2010.
Laird, Elizabeth. *A Fistful of Pearls and Other Tales from Iraq*. London: Frances Lincoln Children's Books, 2008.
Samuels, Charlie. *Iraq*. Washington, D.C.: National Geographic Children's Books, 2007.
Stamaty, Mark Alan. *Alia's Mission: Saving the Books of Iraq*. New York: Dragonfly Books, 2010.
Steele, Phillip. *Mesopotamia*. New York: DK Publishing, 2007.
The War in Iraq: From the Front Lines to the Home Front. New York: Scholastic, 2009.

Works Consulted

BBC News. "Iraq Increases Oil Reserves by 24 Percent." October 4, 2010. http://www.bbc.co.uk/news/business-11468209
The British Museum. "Ziggurats." http://www.mesopotamia.co.uk/ziggurats/index.html
Chandler, Tertius. *Four Thousand Years of Urban Growth: An Historical Census*. Lewiston, NY: The Edwin Mellen Press, 1987.
Ditmars, Hadani. "Culture from Chaos: Where Next for Iraqi Art?" *The Guardian*, March 12, 2010. http://www.guardian.co.uk/artanddesign/2010/mar/12/iraq-war-art-heritage
Fang, Bay. "When Saddam Ruled the Day." *U.S. News & World Report*, July 11, 2004. http://www.usnews.com/usnews/news/articles/040719/19iraq.htm
Fattah, Hala. *A Brief History of Iraq*. New York: Checkmark Books, 2009.
Food and Agriculture Organization of the United Nations. "Top Production—Iraq—2008." http://faostat.fao.org/DesktopDefault.aspx?PageID=339&lang=en&country=103
GlobalSecurity.org. "Iran-Iraq War (1980–1988)." http://www.globalsecurity.org/military/world/war/iran-iraq.htm
Hunt, Courtney. *A History of Iraq*. Westport, CT: Greenwood Press, 2005.
Inter-Agency Information and Analysis Unit. "Education in Iraq." April 2010. http://www.iauiraq.org/reports/mdgs/Education-Factsheet-English-v2.pdf
Internet World Stats. "Middle East Internet Usage Stats and Facebook Statistics." September 20, 2010. http://www.internetworldstats.com/middle.htm#iq
IraqiGirl. *IraqiGirl: Diary of a Teenage Girl in Iraq*. Chicago: Haymarket Books, 2009.
Karim, Kay. "Baked Fish-Samak Maskouf." From *The Iraqi Family Cookbook*. Falls Church, VA: *The Iraqi Family Cookbook*, LLC, 2006. http://iraqifamilycookbook.blogspot.com/2007/06/baked-fish-maskouf.html
Koppes, Clayton R. "Captain Mahan, General Gordon, and the Origins of the Term 'Middle East.' " *Middle Eastern Studies*, vol.12, n. 1, 1976.

Malinowski, Jon C. *Geographic Perspectives: Iraq.* Guilford, CT: McGraw-Hill/Dushkin, 2004.

Munier, Gilles. *Iraq: An Illustrated History and Guide.* Northampton, MA: Interlink Books, 2004.

Nissen, Hans J., and Peter Heine. *From Mesopotamia to Iraq: A Concise History.* Chicago: The University of Chicago Press, 2009.

Pax, Salam. *The Clandestine Diary of an Ordinary Iraqi.* New York: Grove Press, 2003.

Polk, William R. *Understanding Iraq.* New York: HarperCollins, 2005.

Republic of Iraq Ministry of Higher Education and Scientific Research
    http://www.mohesr.gov.iq/EngPages/indexE.htm

Robins, Philip. *The Middle East.* Oxford: OneWorld Publications, 2009.

Rossi, Melissa. *What Every American Should Know About the Middle East.* New York: Penguin Books, 2008.

Shadid, Anthony. "Iraqi Cleric Embraces State in Comeback Speech." *The New York Times,* January 8, 2011. http://www.nytimes.com/2011/01/09/world/middleeast/09iraq.html

Sieff, Martin. *The Politically Incorrect Guide to the Middle East.* Washington, DC: Regenery Publishing, 2008.

Tripp, Charles. *A History of Iraq.* Cambridge, UK: Cambridge University Press, 2000.

University of Pennsylvania Museum of Archaeology and Anthropology. "Write Like a Babylonian." http://www.penn.museum/games/cuneiform.shtml

UN Office of the Iraq Programme Oil-for-Food.
    http://www.un.org/Depts/oip/index.html

U.S. Central Intelligence Agency. *The World Factbook:* "Iraq." February 14, 2011.
    https://www.cia.gov/library/publications/the-world-factbook/geos/iz.html

The World Bank. "Iraq." June 6, 2010. http://web.worldbank.org/WBSITE/EXTERNAL/COUNTRIES/MENAEXT/IRAQEXTN/0,,menuPK:313111~pagePK:141159~piPK:141110~theSitePK:313105,00.html

World Travel Market. "Iraq, the Next Tourism Hot Spot." November 8, 2010.
    http://www.wtmlondon.com/page.cfm?T=m/Action=Press/PressID=1755.

On the Internet
Ancient Mesopotamia: This History, Our History
    http://mesopotamia.lib.uchicago.edu/
Embassy of the Republic of Iraq
    http://www.mofamission.gov.iq/home.aspx
Iraq: Country Facts, Information, Photos, Videos—National Geographic Kids
    http://kids.nationalgeographic.com/kids/places/find/iraq/
IraqiGirl's Blog
    http://iraqigirl.blogspot.com/
Iraq Museum International
    http://www.baghdadmuseum.org
Kurdistan: The Other Iraq
    http://www.theotheriraq.com/

autonomous (aw-TAH-nuh-mus)—Self-governing.

burka (BUR-kah)—Also spelled *burqa,* a loose, long-sleeved robe worn by traditional Muslim women that covers the entire body and face, with a slit or light veil for the eyes.

caliphate (KAL-ih-fayt)—A government headed by an Islamic leader, or caliph.

cartel (kar-TEL)—An international group formed to control prices and production of a good or business in high demand.

citadel (SIH-tih-del)—A strongly fortified place within a city, like a fortress, made to withstand enemy attack.

coup (KOO)—From the French term *coup d'etat* (KOO day-TAH), a sudden and often violent overthrow of a government.

cuneiform (kyoo-NEE-uh-form)—A form of writing invented by the Sumerians around 3000 BCE, made by pressing river reeds into soft clay.

dialect (DYE-uh-lekt)—A form of speaking a standard language with accents and special words.

ethnic group (ETH-nik GROOP)—A group of people that share a distinct culture, religion, or language.

generator (JEN-er-ay-tur)—A machine that uses mechanical energy—from a gasoline-powered motor or a wind turbine, for example—to create electricity.

Hadith (hah-DEETH)—A collection of stories and customs about the Prophet Muhammad and his followers.

imam (ee-MOM)—A Muslim religious leader.

Koran (kor-AN)—The holy book of Islam, believed to be the words of Allah as spoken to his prophet Muhammad.

militia (mih-LIH-shuh)—A group of citizen soldiers called to action during a state of emergency.

minaret (MIH-nuh-ret)—The high, slender tower of a mosque.

Mukhabarat (moo-KAH-bah-rot)—The intelligence-gathering arm of an Arabic government.

sanction (SANK-shun)—A punishment, such as withholding trade goods, used to enforce a law.

Shari'a (shah-REE-uh)—Islamic law based on the Koran, the Hadith, and other sources.

Shiite (SHEE-eyt)—A follower of Shi'a Islam, which says that Islamic religious leaders must be descendants of the Prophet Muhammad.

souk (SOOK)—An open-air market or bazaar, from the Arabic word for "marketplace."

sunnah (SOO-nah)—From the Arabic word for "way" or "path," the Muslim guide for righteous living, based on the Koran and stories of Muhammad's life.

Sunni (SOO-nee)—A follower of Sunni Islam, which believes that Islamic religious leaders need not be direct descendants of the Prophet Muhammad, but rather can be chosen by a council called a *shura.*

totalitarian (toh-tal-ih-TAYR-ee-un)—A government that seeks to control every aspect of life and does not tolerate opposition.

UNESCO (yoo-NESS-koh)—The *U*nited *N*ations *E*ducational, *S*cientific and *C*ultural *O*rganization. A group within the United Nations that promotes and preserves natural and human-made resources around the globe.

wadi (WAH-dee)—A river carved by rainy-season floods that is dry most of the year.

weapons of mass destruction (WMDs)—Weapons that act over a wide area to kill or injure, such as nuclear bombs, chemical weapons such as poison gas, and biological weapons that cause disease.

ziggurat (ZIH-gur-ot)—An enormous, stepped pyramid built by the ancient Sumerians and used as a temple.

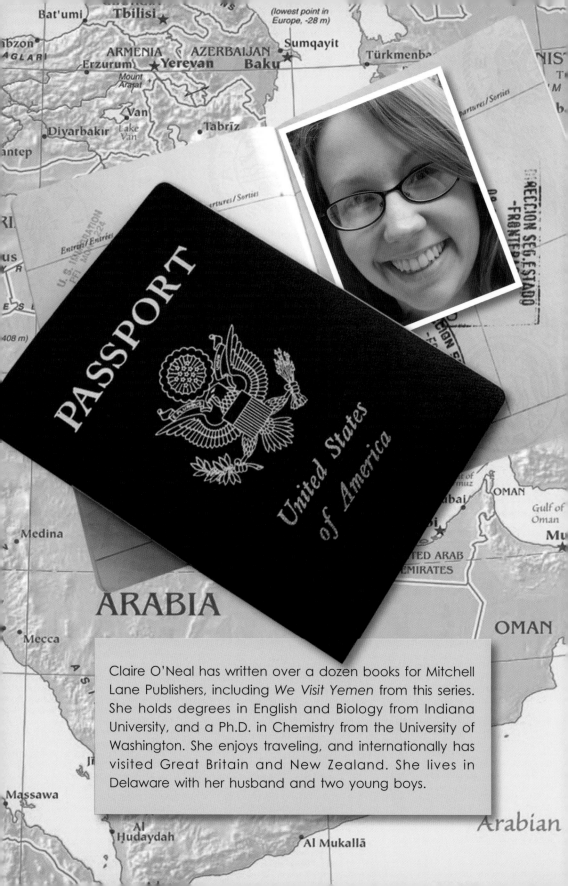

Claire O'Neal has written over a dozen books for Mitchell Lane Publishers, including *We Visit Yemen* from this series. She holds degrees in English and Biology from Indiana University, and a Ph.D. in Chemistry from the University of Washington. She enjoys traveling, and internationally has visited Great Britain and New Zealand. She lives in Delaware with her husband and two young boys.